Computer Manual of a Different Sort

A Collection of Emails You Can Read—
without Fear of a Virus!

ELLEN WEBER NEWLIN

ISBN 979-8-89112-689-3 (Paperback)
ISBN 979-8-89112-690-9 (Digital)

Copyright © 2024 Ellen Weber Newlin
All rights reserved
First Edition

All rights reserved. No part of this publication may be reproduced, distributed, or transmitted in any form or by any means, including photocopying, recording, or other electronic or mechanical methods without the prior written permission of the publisher. For permission requests, solicit the publisher via the address below.

Covenant Books
11661 Hwy 707
Murrells Inlet, SC 29576
www.covenantbooks.com

The computer age brought vast information to anyone who could use a computer. There were many manuals for various programs.

I compiled this "resource" book to hopefully relieve stress. Read it and relax. It includes emails you or your friends may have received or may have sent. Either way, this will be an enjoyable, easy-reading book full of chuckles, laughs, and contemplative materials—without fear of a virus!

Everything in this book has been copied. None of it is original (except this page, of course). The information came from emails. It is not known who originally wrote the emails, and I do *not* claim to have created any of them.

However, the book is my idea; the arrangement of the material is original, and I have put in many hours accumulating the emails into this easy-reading format.

Life is good! Take a break and enjoy.

> A merry heart doeth good like a medicine,
> but a broken spirit drieth the bones.
> —Proverbs 17:22

CONTENTS

Chapter 1: There's No Place Like Home 1
   Mean moms 1
   "Old" is when… 2
   Blondes are back again 2
   Top 10 things only women understand 4
   Ways to know if you have PMS 4
   You know you're on the West Coast when… 4
   You know you're in Alaska when… 5
   You know you're in the South when… 5
   You know you're in Colorado when… 5
   You know you're in the Midwest when… 5
   Dad jokes 6

Chapter 2: Woe Is Me 9
   AAADD 9
   Exercising 10
   Seeing is believing? 11
   Makes sense to me 11
   For safety's sake… 12
   Chicken 12
   Weird things you might never know 13
   Idiots 14
   This 'n' that 15
   Gandhi 17
   How to be annoying 17
   A little humor 20

  Silly questions by silly lawyers 21
  Why some Americans should never be allowed to travel 26
  Deep thoughts 28

Chapter 3: Office Humor 31
  What to say if you're caught sleeping at your desk! 31
  Huh? 32
  You know you are drinking too much coffee when… 33
  So you want the day off? 34
  Get to work! 34
  Office pranks for the insane 35
  Technology for countryfolk 37
  Computer reasoning? 37

Chapter 4: On a Religious Note 39
  Wake-up prayer 39
  Thank you, Lord 39
  Prayers of the stress impaired 40
  Dear God 41
  16 books of the Bible 47
  Kids 'n' religion 48
  Hymns 49
  Letters to pastors 50
  Good instructions 54
  Bible questions 55
  Christian flying 58
  Bulletin bloopers! 58
  The preacher and the song leader 61

Chapter 5: Something to Think About 63
  Ethical questions 63
  Isn't it funny… 64
  Keep your fork! 65
  The four stages of life… 67
  The paradox of our time 67
  Positive attitude 68

Rare works of art	70
Things learned from children	72
The pumpkin	73
All I need to know about life I learned from a cow	73
Everything I need to know about life I learned from Noah's ark	74
Insights	74
Great truths about life	76
Great truths about growing old…	77
Kids' instructions on life	77
Today is a gift	81
The empty egg	81
Life is good	84
Little tidbits	85

CHAPTER 1

There's No Place Like Home

Mean moms

We had the meanest mother in the whole world! While other kids ate candy for breakfast, we had to have cereal, eggs, and toast. When others had a Pepsi and a Twinkie for lunch, we had to eat sandwiches. And you can guess our mother fixed us a dinner that was different from what other kids had too.

Mother insisted on knowing where we were at all times. You'd think we were convicts in a prison. She had to know who our friends were and what we were doing with them. She insisted that if we said we would be gone for an hour, we would be gone for an hour or less.

We were ashamed to admit it, but she had the nerve to break the Child Labor Laws by making us work. We had to wash the dishes, make the beds, learn to cook, vacuum the floor, do laundry, and do all sorts of cruel jobs. I think she would lie awake at night thinking of more things for us to do.

She always insisted on us telling the truth, the whole truth, and nothing but the truth. By the time we were teenagers, she could read our minds. Then life was really tough! Mother wouldn't let our friends just honk the horn when they drove up. They had to come up to the door so she could meet them. While everyone else could date when they were twelve or thirteen, we had to wait until we were sixteen.

Because of our mother, we missed out on lots of things other kids experienced. Few of us have ever been caught shoplifting, vandalizing other's property, or ever arrested for any crime. It was all her fault.

Now that we have left home, we are mostly God-fearing, educated, honest adults. We are doing our best to be mean parents, just like Mom was. I think that's what's wrong with the world today. It just doesn't have enough mean moms anymore.

"Old" is when...

- The birthday candles cost more than the cake.
- You see expensive antiques and you remember one just like it that you threw away.
- You've been there and done that but don't remember what that was.
- Your friends compliment you on your new alligator shoes, and you're barefoot.
- You don't care where your spouse goes as long as you don't have to go along.
- When you are cautioned to slow down by the doctor instead of by the police.
- People tell you how good you look.
- An "all-nighter" means not having to get up at night to "potty."

Blondes are back again

How did the blonde break her leg raking leaves?
She fell out of the tree.
How did the blonde die drinking milk?
The cow stepped on her.
How did the blonde burn her nose?
Bobbing for French fries.
Why do blondes have more fun?
They are easier to amuse.

What do you call twenty blondes in a freezer?
Frosted flakes.
What do you see when you look into a blonde's eyes?
The back of her head.
Why can't blondes put in light bulbs?
They keep breaking them with the hammer.
Did you hear about the blonde who shot an arrow into the air?
She missed.
Why shouldn't blondes have coffee breaks?
It takes too long to retrain them.
What do you call an eternity?
Four blondes at a four-way stop.
How do you confuse a blonde?
Give her a package of M&M's and tell her to put them in alphabetical order.
Why does it say TGIF on a blonde's shoes?
Toes go in first.
Why do blondes smile when they see lightning?
They think their picture is being taken.
Why did the blonde return her new scarf?
It was too tight.
Why did the blonde put makeup on her forehead?
She wanted everyone to know that she was able to make up her mind.
Why did the blonde lose her job as an elevator operator?
She couldn't learn the route.
Why did the blonde drive around the block fifty-seven times?
Her turn signal was stuck.
Why did the blonde ask her friends to save their burned-out light bulbs?
She needed them for the darkroom she was building.
What is the biggest advantage of marrying a blonde?
You get to park in the Handicapped Zone.
What do you call twenty blondes in a circle?
A dope ring.
What do you call a blonde who's dyed her hair brown?
Artificial Intelligence.

Top 10 things only women understand

10. Cats' facial expressions.
9. The need for the same style of shoes in different colors.
8. Why bean sprouts aren't just weeds.
7. Fat clothes.
6. Taking a car trip without trying to beat your best time.
5. The difference between beige, off-white, and eggshell.
4. Cutting your bangs to make them grow.
3. Eyelash curlers.
2. The inaccuracy of every bathroom scale ever made.

And the number one thing only women understand…

1. Other women!

Ways to know if you have PMS

- Everyone around you has an attitude problem.
- You're adding chocolate chips to your cheese omelet.
- The dryer has shrunk every last pair of your jeans.
- Your husband is suddenly agreeing to everything you say.
- You're using your cell phone to dial up every bumper sticker that says, "How's my driving? Call 1-800-***-****."
- Everyone's head looks like an invitation to batting practice.
- You're sure that everyone is scheming to drive you crazy.
- The ibuprofen bottle is empty, and you bought it yesterday.

You know you're on the West Coast when…

- You make more than $250,000 and still can't afford to buy your own house.
- The high school quarterback calls a time-out to answer his cell phone.
- The fastest part of your commute is going down your driveway.
- You know how to eat an artichoke.
- You drive to your neighborhood block party.

COMPUTER MANUAL OF A DIFFERENT SORT

You know you're in Alaska when...

- You only have four spices: salt, pepper, ketchup, and Tabasco.
- Halloween costumes fit over parkas.
- You have more than one recipe for moose.
- The four seasons are winter, still winter, almost winter, and construction.

You know you're in the South when...

- You can get a movie and bait in the same store.
- "Y'all" is singular, and "all y'all" is plural.
- After a year, you still hear, "Y'all ain't from 'round here, are ya?"
- "He needed killin'" is a valid defense.

You know you're in Colorado when...

- You carry your $3,000 mountain bike atop your $500 car.
- You tell your husband to pick up Granola on his way home, and he stops at the daycare center to pick up your child.
- A pass does not involve a football or dating.

You know you're in the Midwest when...

- You've never met any celebrities, but the mayor knows your name.
- Your idea of a traffic jam is ten cars waiting to pass a tractor.
- You have had to switch from "heat" to "A/C" on the same day.
- You end sentences with a preposition: "Where's my coat at?" or "If you go to the mall, I wanna go with."
- Your first job was detasseling corn.
- When asked how your trip was to any exotic place, you say, "It was different."

- You consult the football schedule before planning your wedding date.

Dad jokes

How many telemarketers does it take to change a light bulb?
Only one, but he has to do it while you are eating dinner.
How many DIY buffs does it take to change a light bulb?
One, but it takes two weeks and four trips to the hardware store.
How many paranoids does it take to change a light bulb?
Who wants to know?
I was addicted to the Hokey Pokey, but I turned myself around.
I don't trust stairs. They are always up to something.
Today, my son asked, "Can I have a bookmark?" I burst into tears. Eleven years old, and he still doesn't know my name is Brian.
Why didn't Han Solo enjoy his steak dinner?
It was Chewie.
Why don't pirates take a bath before they walk the plank?
They just wash up on shore.
Did you hear about the racing snail who got rid of his shell?
He thought it would make him faster, but it just made him sluggish.
Did you hear about the guy who froze to death at the drive-in?
He went to see "Closed for the Winter."
We all know about Murphy's Law: anything that can go wrong will go wrong. But have you heard of Cole's Law?
It's thinly sliced cabbage.
When does a joke become a "dad joke?"
When it becomes apparent.
"Knock, knock." "Who's there?" "Nobel." "Nobel who?" "Nobel, so I knock knocked."
"Knock, knock." "Who's there?" "Alabama." "Anybody with you?" "Nope. I'm Alabama self."
"Knock, knock." "Who's there?" "Ayatollah." "Ayatollah who?" "Ayatollah you already."

Did you hear about the kidnapping at school?
No. What happened?
The teacher woke him up.
What's the least spoken language in the world?
Sign language.
What do you call a hippie's wife?
Mississippi.

I searched for a lighter on Amazon, but all I could find was 401 matches.

I sold our vacuum cleaner. It was just gathering dust.

What did the DNA say to the other DNA?
"Do these genes make me look fat?"
What do you need to make a small fortune on Wall Street?
A large fortune.
How does the man in the moon get his hair cut?
Eclipse it.

Did you hear about the restaurant on the moon? Great food, no atmosphere!

I spent a lot of time, money, and effort childproofing my house, but the kids still get in.

CHAPTER 2

Woe Is Me

AAADD

I have recently been diagnosed with AAADD: age-activated attention-deficit disorder. This is how it goes.

I decide to change the oil in the car, so I go to the garage and notice the mail on the table. Okay, I'm going to work on the car. *But first*, I'm going to go through the mail. I lay the car keys down on the desk.

After discarding the junk mail, I noticed the trashcan was full. Okay, I'll just put the bills on my desk. *But first*, I'll take the trash out—but since I'm going to be near the mailbox, I'll address a few bills... Yes, now where is the checkbook?

Oops...there's only one check left. Where did I put the extra checks? Oh, there is my empty plastic cup from last night on my desk. I'm going to look for those checks... *But first*, I need to put the cup back in the kitchen.

I head for the kitchen, look out the window, and notice the flowers need a drink of water. I put the cup on the counter, and there's my extra pair of glasses on the kitchen counter. What are they doing here? I'll just put them away... *But first*, I need to water those plants. I head for the door and—

Aaaagh! Someone left the TV remote in the wrong spot. Okay, I'll put the remote away and water the plants… *But first*, I need to find those checks.

At the end of the day, oil in the car is still not changed, bills are still unpaid, cup is still in the sink, and the checkbook still has only one check left. I lost my car keys; and when I try to figure out how come nothing got done today, I'm baffled. Because *I know I was busy all day*! I realize this condition is serious. I'd get help, *but first*, I think I'll check my email.

Exercising

- It is well-documented that for every minute you exercise, you add one minute to your life. This enables you, at eighty-five years old, to spend an additional five months in a nursing home at $5,000 per month.
- My grandmother started walking five miles a day when she was sixty. Now she's ninety-seven years old, and we don't know where the heck she is.
- I joined a health club last year, spent about 400 bucks, and haven't lost a pound. Apparently, you have to show up.
- I have to exercise early in the morning before my brain figures out what I'm doing.
- I like long walks, especially when people who annoy me take them.
- I have flabby thighs, but fortunately, my stomach covers them.
- The advantage of exercising every day is that you die healthier.
- If you are going to try cross-country skiing, start with a small country.

Seeing is believing?

> My face in the mirror
> Isn't wrinkled or drawn.
> My house isn't dirty,
> The cobwebs are gone.
> My garden looks lovely
> And so does my lawn.
> I think I might never
> Put my glasses back on.
>
> —Author Unknown

Makes sense to me

- Save the whales. Collect a whole set.
- A day without sunshine is like…night.
- On the other hand, you have different fingers.
- I just got lost in thought. It was unfamiliar territory.
- I feel like I'm diagonally parked in a parallel universe.
- Honk if you love peace and quiet.
- He who laughs last thinks slowest.
- Depression is merely anger without enthusiasm.
- Monday is an awful way to spend 1/7 of your week.
- A clear conscience is usually the sign of a bad memory.
- Okay, so what's the speed of dark?
- If everything seems to be going well, you have obviously overlooked something.
- I couldn't repair your brakes, so I made your horn louder.
- Inside every older person is a younger person wondering what happened.
- You are unique, just like everyone else.

For safety's sake...

- Do *not* ride in automobiles: they cause 20 percent of all fatal accidents.
- Do *not* stay home: 17 percent of all accidents occur in the home.
- Do *not* walk on the streets or sidewalks: 14 percent of all accidents happen to pedestrians.
- Do *not* travel by air, rail, or water: 16 percent of all accidents happen on these.
- Only .001 percent of all deaths occur in worship services in church, and these are related to previous physical disorders. Hence, the safest place for you to be at any time is church. Bible study is safe too. The percentage there is even less. Go to church! It could save your life!

Chicken

In 1994, scientists developed a gun built specifically to launch dead chickens at the windshields of airliners, military jets, and the space shuttle, all traveling at maximum velocity. The idea is to simulate the frequent incidents of collisions with airborne fowl to test the strength of aerospace windshields. British engineers heard about the gun and were eager to test it on the windshields of their new high-speed trains. Arrangements were made to borrow the gun. But when the gun was fired, the engineers stood shocked as the chicken hurtled out of the barrel, crashed into the shatterproof shield, smashed it to smithereens, crashed through the control console, snapped the engineer's backrest in two, and embedded itself in the back wall of the cabin.

Horrified, the British sent the disastrous results of the experiment, along with the designs of the windshield, and begged the US scientists for suggestions. The scientists emailed a response of just one sentence: "Thaw the chicken."

Weird things you might never know
(according to emails prior to 2002)

- Butterflies taste with their feet.
- A duck's quack doesn't echo.
- In ten minutes, a hurricane releases more energy than all the world's nuclear weapons combined.
- On average, one hundred people choke to death on ball-point pens every year.
- On average, people fear spiders more than they do death.
- Ninety percent of New York City cabbies are recently arrived immigrants.
- Thirty-five percent of the people who use personal ads for dating are already married.
- Elephants are the only animals that can't jump.
- Only one person in two billion will live to be 116 or older.
- It's possible to lead a cow upstairs…but not downstairs.
- Women blink nearly twice as much as men.
- The main library at Indiana University sinks over an inch every year because when it was built, engineers failed to take into account the weight of all the books that would occupy the building.
- A snail can sleep for three years.
- No word in the English language rhymes with "month."
- The average life span of a major league baseball is seven pitches.
- Our eyes are always the same size from birth, but our noses and ears never stop growing.
- A dentist invented the electric chair.
- All polar bears are left-handed.
- In ancient Egypt, priests plucked *every* hair from their bodies, including their eyebrows and eyelashes.
- An ostrich's eye is bigger than its brain.
- "Typewriter" is the longest word that can be made using the letters on only one row of the keyboard.

- "Go" is the shortest complete sentence in the English language.
- If Barbie were life-size, her measurements would be 39-23-33. She would stand seven feet, two inches tall.
- A crocodile cannot stick its tongue out.
- The cigarette lighter was invented before the match.
- Americans, on average, eat eighteen acres of pizza every day.

Idiots

At work I was signing the receipt for my credit card purchase when the clerk noticed I had never signed my name on the back of the credit card. She informed me she could not complete the transaction unless the card was signed. When I asked why, she said she must compare the signature on the credit card with the signature I just signed on the receipt. So I signed the credit card in front of her. She carefully compared the signature to the one I had just signed on the receipt. As luck would have it, they matched.

In the neighborhood. I live in a semirural area. We recently had a new neighbor call the local township administrative office to request the removal of the Deer Crossing sign on our road. The reason: too many deer were hit by cars, and he no longer wanted them to cross there.

In food service. My daughter went to a local Taco Bell and ordered a taco. She asked the individual behind the counter for "minimal lettuce." He said he was sorry, but they only had iceberg.

At the airport. I was checking in at the gate at the airport when the airport employee asked, "Has anyone put anything in your baggage without your knowledge?" I said, "If it was without my knowledge, how would I know?" He smiled and nodded knowingly, "That's why we ask."

On the road. The stoplight on the corner buzzes when it is safe to cross the street. I was crossing with an intellectually challenged coworker of mine when she asked if I knew what the buzzer was for. I explain that it signals blind people when the light is red. She responded, appalled, "What on earth are blind people doing driving?"

In management. At a goodbye lunch for an old and dear coworker who is leaving the company due to "downsizing," our manager spoke up and said, "This is fun. We should have lunch like this more often." Not another word was spoken. We just looked at each other like deer staring into the headlights of an approaching truck.

With computers. I worked with an individual who plugged her power strip back into itself, and for the life of her, she could not understand why her system would not turn on.

In general. When my husband and I arrived at an automobile dealership to pick up our car, we were told that the keys had been accidentally locked in it. We went to the service department and found a mechanic working feverishly to unlock the driver's side door. As I watched from the passenger's side, I instinctively tried the door handle and discovered it was open. "Hey," I announced to the technician, "it's open." The young man answered, "I already got that side."

This 'n' that

A phone company fired its president after nine months, saying he lacked "intellectual leadership." He received a $26 million severance package. Perhaps it's not the president who lacks intelligence.

*****

Police in a city in California spent two hours attempting to subdue a gunman who had barricaded himself inside his home. After firing ten tear gas canisters, officers discovered that the man was standing beside them, shouting, "Please come out and give yourself up!"

*****

An Illinois man, pretending to have a gun, kidnapped a motorist, forcing him to drive to two different automated teller machines.

The kidnapper then proceeded to withdraw money from his own bank accounts.

*****

A man walked into a Kansas convenience store and asked for all the money in the cash drawer. Apparently, the take was too small, so he tied up the store clerk and worked the counter himself for three hours until police showed up and grabbed him.

*****

Police in Los Angeles had good luck with a robbery suspect who just couldn't control himself during a lineup. When detectives asked each man in the lineup to repeat the words, "Give me all your money, or I'll shoot." The man shouted, "That's not what I said!"

*****

A man spoke frantically into the phone, "My wife is pregnant, and her contractions are only two minutes apart!"
"Is this her first child?" the doctor asked.
"No!" the man shouted. "This is her husband!"

*****

In California, a man was arrested for trying to hold up a bank branch without a weapon. He used a thumb and a finger to simulate a gun, but unfortunately, he failed to keep his hand in his pocket.

*****

On a lake located in the high desert, an hour east of Bakersfield, California, some folks, new to boating, were having a problem. No matter how hard they tried, they couldn't get their brand-new twenty-two-foot Bayliner to perform. It wouldn't get on a plane at all, and it was very sluggish in almost every maneuver, no matter how much power was applied. After about an hour of trying to make it go, they pulled over to a nearby marina, thinking someone there could tell them what was wrong. A thorough topside check revealed everything in perfect working order. The engine ran fine, the outdrive went up and down, and the prop was the correct size and pitch. So one of the marina guys jumped in the water to check underneath. He came up choking on water. He was laughing so hard. Remember, this is supposedly a true story. Under the boat, still strapped securely in place, was the trailer.

Gandhi

Mahatma Gandhi, as you know, walked barefoot most of the time. This produced an impressive set of calluses on his feet. He also ate very little, which made him rather frail, and with his odd diet, he suffered from bad breath. This made him what?
Answer: *A super-callused, fragile mystic plagued with halitosis.*

How to be annoying

- Adjust the tint on your TV so that all the people are green, and insist to others that you "like it that way."
- Sing the Batman theme incessantly.
- Staple papers in the middle of the page.
- Produce a rental video consisting entirely of FBI copy warnings.
- Sew anti-theft detector strips into people's backpacks.
- Hide dairy products in inaccessible places.
- Specify that your drive-through order is "to go."
- Honk and wave to strangers.
- Dress only in clothes colored Hunter's Orange.
- Change channels five minutes before the end of every show.
- Begin all your sentences with "ooh-la-la!"
- Leave someone's printer in the compressed-italic-Cyrillic-landscape mode.

- ONLY TYPE IN UPPERCASE.
- only type in lowercase.
- Don't use any punctuation either
- Tie jingle bells to all your clothes.
- Repeat everything someone says as a question.
- Repeat everything someone says as a question?
- Inform everyone you meet of your personal Kennedy assassination, UFO, and O. J. Simpson conspiracy theories.
- Repeat the following conversation a dozen times: "Do you hear that? What? Never mind, it's gone now."
- Push all the flat Lego pieces together tightly.
- When Christmas caroling, sing "Jingle Bells, Batman smells," until physically restrained.
- Wear a cape that says "Magnificent One."
- As much as possible, skip rather than walk.
- Stand over someone's shoulder, mumbling as they read.
- Finish the ninety-nine bottles of beer song.
- Sing the "This is the song that never ends" song.
- Leave your turn signal on for fifty miles.
- Pretend your mouse is a CB radio, and talk to it.
- Try playing the William Tell Overture by tapping on the bottom of your chin. When nearly done, announce, "No, wait, I messed it up," and repeat.
- Drive half a block.
- Name your dog "Dog."
- Inform others that they exist only in your imagination.
- Reply to everything someone says with "That's what YOU think."
- Lick the filling out of all sandwich cookies, and place the cookie parts back in the tray.
- Cultivate a Norwegian accent. If Norwegian, affect a Southern Drawl.
- Forget the punch line to a long joke, but assure the listener it was a real hoot.

- Routinely handcuff yourself to furniture, informing the curious that you don't want to fall off "in case the big one comes."
- Follow a few paces behind someone, spraying everything they touch with a can of disinfectant.
- Deliberately hum songs that will remain lodged in coworkers' brains, such as "Feliz Navidad," "Green Acres," or Mr. Roger's Theme song.
- While making presentations, occasionally bob your head like a parakeet.
- Lie obviously about trivial things such as the time of day.
- Sit in your front yard, pointing a hair dryer at passing cars to see if they slow down.
- Invent nonsense computer jargon in conversations, and see if people play along to avoid the appearance of ignorance.
- Sing along at the opera.
- Finish all your sentences with the words "in accordance with prophecy."
- Ask the waitress for an extra seat for your "imaginary friend."
- Go to a poetry recital and ask why each poem doesn't rhyme.
- Ask your coworkers mysterious questions, and scribble their answers in a notebook.
- Incessantly recite annoying phrases, such as "sticky wicket isn't cricket."
- Select the same song on the jukebox fifty times.
- Do not add any inflection to the end of your sentences, producing awkward silences with the impression that you'll be saying more at any moment.
- Never make eye contact.
- Never break eye contact.
- Signal that a conversation is over by clamping your hands over your ears.
- Holler random numbers while someone is counting.
- Make appointments for the thirty-first of September.

- Invite lots of people to other people's parties.

A little humor

A man is in bed with his wife when there is a rat-a-tat-tat on the door. He rolls over and looks at his clock, and it is half past three in the morning.

"I'm not getting out of bed at this time," he thinks and rolls over. Then a louder knock follows.

"Aren't you going to answer that?" says his wife. So, he drags himself out of bed and goes downstairs. He opens the door, and there is a man standing at the door. It didn't take the homeowner long to realize the man was drunk.

"Hi there," slurs the stranger. "Can you give me a push?"

"No, get lost. It's half past three. I was in bed," says the man and slams the door.

He goes back up to bed and tells his wife what happened, and she says, "Dave, that wasn't very nice of you. Remember that night we broke down in the pouring rain on the way to pick the kids up from the babysitter, and you had to knock on that man's house to get us started again? What would have happened if he'd told us to get lost?"

"But the guy was drunk," says the husband.

"It doesn't matter," says the wife. "He needs our help, and it would be the Christian thing to help him."

So the husband gets out of bed again, gets dressed, and goes downstairs. He opens the door, and not being able to see the stranger anywhere, he shouts, "Hey, do you still want a push?"

And he hears a voice cry out, "Yeah, please."

So still, being unable to see the stranger, he shouts, "Where are you?"

And the stranger replies, "I'm over here on your swing."

*****

Joe Smith started the day early, having set his alarm clock (made in Japan) for 6:00 a.m. While his coffeepot (made in Japan) is perking, he puts his blow dryer (made in Taiwan) to work and shaves with his electric razor (made in Hong Kong). He puts on a dress shirt (made in Taiwan), designer jeans (made in Singapore), and a pair of tennis shoes (made in Korea).

After cooking up some breakfast in his new electric skillet (made in the Philippines), he sits down to figure out on his calculator (made in Mexico) how much he can spend today. After setting his watch (made in Switzerland) to the radio (made in Hong Kong), he goes out, gets in his car (made in Germany), and, as has been his daily task for months, goes looking for a good-paying American job.

After the end of another discouraging and fruitless day, Joe decides to relax for a while. He puts on a pair of sandals (made in Brazil), pours himself a glass of wine (made in France), turns on his TV (made in Japan), and ponders again why he can't find that "good-paying American job."

*****

A middle-aged woman has a heart attack. While on the operating table, she has a near-death experience. She sees God and asks, "Is this it? Am I dead?"

God says, "No, you have another thirty to forty years to live."

She recovers and decides to stay in the hospital and have a facelift, liposuction, breast augmentation, tummy tuck, hair dyed, and so on. She figures since she's got another thirty to forty years, she might as well make the most of it.

She walks out of the hospital after the last operation and immediately gets hit by an ambulance. She arrives in front of God and asks, "I thought you said I had another thirty to forty years?" God replies, "Sorry, I didn't recognize you."

Silly questions by silly lawyers

Q: What is your date of birth?

A: July 15.
Q: What year?
A: Every year.

*****

Q: What gear were you in at the moment of the impact?
A: Gucci sweats and Reeboks.

*****

Q: How old is your son, the one living with you?
A: Thirty-eight or thirty-five, I can't remember which.
Q: How long has he lived with you?
A: Forty-five years.

*****

Q: And where was the location of the accident?
A: Approximately milepost 499.
Q: And where is milepost 499?
A: Probably between milepost 498 and 500.

*****

Q: Did you blow your horn or anything?
A: After the accident?
Q: Before the accident.
A: Sure, I played for ten years. I even went to school for it.

*****

Q: Sir, what is your IQ?
A: Well, I can see pretty well, I think.

*****

COMPUTER MANUAL OF A DIFFERENT SORT

Q: Trooper, when you stopped the defendant, were your red and blue lights flashing?
A: Yes.
Q: Did the defendant say anything when she got out of her car?
A: Yes, sir.
Q: What did she say?
A: What disco am I at?

*****

Q: Now, Doctor, isn't it true that when a person dies in his sleep, he doesn't know about it until the next morning?

*****

Q: The youngest son, the twenty-year-old, how old is he?

*****

Q: Were you present when your picture was taken?

*****

Q: Was it you or your younger brother who was killed in the war?

*****

Q: Did he kill you?

*****

Q: How far apart were the vehicles at the time of the collision?

*****

Q: You were there until the time you left. Is that true?

*****

Q: How many times have you committed suicide?

*****

Q: She had three children, right?
A: Yes.
Q: How many were boys?
A: None.
Q: Were there any girls?

*****

Q: You say the stairs went down to the basement?
A: Yes.
Q: And these stairs, did they go up also?

*****

Q: Mr. Slattery, you went on a rather elaborate honeymoon, didn't you?
A: I went to Europe, sir.
Q: And you took your new wife?

*****

Q: Are you qualified to give a urine sample?

*****

Q: How was your first marriage terminated?
A: By death.

COMPUTER MANUAL OF A DIFFERENT SORT

Q: And by whose death was it terminated?

*****

Q: Is your appearance here this morning pursuant to a deposition notice that I sent to your attorney?
A: No, this is how I dress when I go to work.

*****

Q: Doctor, how many autopsies have you performed on dead people?
A: All my autopsies are performed on dead people.

*****

Q: Doctor, before you performed the autopsy, did you check for a pulse?
A: No.
Q: Did you check for blood pressure?
A: No.
Q: Did you check for breathing?
A: No.
Q: So then it is possible that the patient was alive when you began the autopsy?
A: No.
Q: How can you be so sure, Doctor?
A: Because his brain was sitting on my desk in a jar.
Q: But could the patient have still been alive nevertheless?
A: It is possible that he could have been alive and practicing law somewhere.

*****

Q: All your responses must be oral, okay? What school did you go to?

A: Oral.

*****

Q: Do you recall the time that you examined the body?
A: The autopsy started around 8:30 p.m.
Q: And Mr. Smith was dead at the time?
A: No, he was sitting on the table wondering why I was doing an autopsy.

Why some Americans should never be allowed to travel

Stories provided by travel agents via the internet

- I had someone ask for an aisle seat on the plane so their hair wouldn't get messed up by being near the window.
- A client called inquiring about a package to Hawaii. After going over all the cost information, she asked, "Would it be cheaper to fly to California and then take the train to Hawaii?
- I got a call from a woman who wanted to go to Capetown. I started to explain the length of the flight and the passport information when she interrupted me with, "I'm not trying to make you look stupid, but Capetown is in Massachusetts." Without trying to make her look stupid, I calmly explained, "Cape Cod is in Massachusetts, Capetown, is in Africa." Her response? *Click*.
- A man called, furious about a Florida package we did. I asked what was wrong with the vacation in Orlando. He said he was expecting an ocean-view room. I tried to explain that it was not possible since Orlando was in the middle of the state. He replied, "Don't lie to me. I looked on the map, and Florida is a very thin state."
- I got a call from a man who asked, "Is it possible to see England from Canada?" I said, "No." He said, "But they look so close on the map."

COMPUTER MANUAL OF A DIFFERENT SORT

- A man called and asked if he could rent a car in Dallas. When I pulled up the reservation, I noticed he had a one-hour layover in Dallas. When I asked him why he wanted to rent a car, he said, "I heard Dallas was a big airport, and I need a car to drive between the gates to save time."
- A nice lady just called. She needed to know how it was possible that her flight from Detroit left at 8:20 a.m. and got into Chicago at 8:33 a.m. I tried to explain that Michigan was an hour ahead of Illinois, but she could not understand the concept of time zones. Finally, I told her the plane went very fast, and she bought that!
- A woman called and asked, "Do airlines put your physical description on your bag so they know whose luggage belongs to whom?" I said, "No, why do you ask?" She replied, "Well, when I checked in with the airline, they put a tag on my luggage that said FAT, and I'm overweight. Is there any connection?" After putting her on hold for a minute while I "looked into it" (I was actually laughing), I came back and explained the city code for Fresno is FAT and that the airline was just putting a destination tag on her luggage.
- I just got off the phone with a man who asked, "How do I know which plane to get on?" I asked what exactly he meant, and he replied, "I was told my flight number is 823, but none of these planes have numbers on them.'
- A woman called saying, "I need to fly to Pepsi-Cola on one of those computer planes." I asked if she meant Pensacola on a commuter plane. She replied, "Yeah, whatever."
- A businessman called and had a question about the documents he needed to fly to China. After a lengthy discussion about passports, I reminded him he needed a visa. "Oh no, I don't. I've been to China many times and never had to have one of those." I double-checked, and sure enough, his stay required a visa. When I told him this, he said, "Look, I've been to China four times, and every time they have accepted my American Express."

- A woman called to make reservations, "I want to go from Chicago to Hippopotamus, New York." The agent was at a loss for words. Finally, the agent asked, "Are you sure that's the name of the town?" "Yes, what flights do you have?" replied the customer. After some searching, the agent came back with, "I'm sorry, ma'am. I've looked up every airport code in the country and can't find a Hippopotamus anywhere." The customer retorted, "Oh, don't be silly. Everyone knows where it is. Check your map!" The agent scoured a map of the state of New York and finally offered, "You don't mean Buffalo, do you?" "That's it! I knew it was a big animal!"

Deep thoughts

- Last night, I played a blank tape at full blast. The mime next door went nuts.
- If a person with multiple personalities threatens suicide, is that considered a hostage situation?
- Just think how much deeper the ocean would be if sponges didn't live there.
- If a cow laughed, would milk come out her nose?
- Whatever happened to preparations A through G?
- If olive oil comes from olives, where does baby oil come from?
- I went for a walk last night, and my kids asked me how long I'd be gone. I said, 'The whole time.'
- How come you don't ever hear about gruntled employees? And who has been dissing them anyhow?
- After eating, do amphibians need to wait an hour to get OUT of the water?
- Why don't they just make mouse-flavored cat food?
- If you are sending someone some Styrofoam, what do you pack it in?
- I just got skylights put in my place. The people who live above me are furious.

- Why do they sterilize needles for lethal injections?
- Do they have reserved parking for non-handicapped people at the Special Olympics?
- Is it true that cannibals don't eat clowns because they taste funny?
- If it's tourist season, why can't we shoot them?
- Since light travels faster than sound, isn't that why some people appear bright until you hear them speak?
- How come abbreviated is such a long word?
- If it's zero degrees outside today and it's supposed to be twice as cold tomorrow, how cold is it going to be?
- Why do you press harder on a remote control when you know the battery is dead?
- Since Americans throw rice at weddings, do Asians throw hamburgers?
- Why are they called buildings when they're already finished? Shouldn't they be called builts?
- Why are they called apartments when they're all stuck together?
- Why do banks charge you a "nonsufficient funds fee" on money they already know you don't have?
- If the universe is everything, and scientists say that the universe is expanding, what is it expanding into?
- If I got into a cab, and the guy started driving backward, would the taxi driver end up owing me money?
- What would a chair look like if your knees bent the other way?
- Why is a carrot more orange than an orange?
- When two airplanes almost collide, why do they call it a near miss? It sounds like a near hit to me!
- Do fish get cramps after eating?
- Why are there five syllables in the word "monosyllabic"?
- Why do they call it the Department of Interior when they are in charge of everything outdoors?
- Why do scientists call it research when looking for something new?

CHAPTER 3

Office Humor

What to say if you're caught sleeping at your desk!

- They told me at the blood bank this might happen.
- This is just a fifteen-minute power nap like they raved about in the last time-management course you sent me to.
- Whew! Guess I left the top off the liquid paper.
- I was meditating on the mission statement and envisioning a new paradigm.
- This is one of the seven habits of highly effective people.
- I was testing the keyboard for drool resistance.
- I was doing a highly specific Yoga exercise to relieve work-related stress. Are you discriminating against people who practice yoga?
- I was doing a "Stress Level Elimination Exercise Plan" (SLEEP) that I learned at the last mandatory seminar you made me go to.
- Why did you interrupt me? I had almost figured out a solution to our biggest problem.
- The coffee machine is broken.
- Someone must have put the decaf in the wrong pot.
- Boy, that cold medicine I took last night just won't wear off!

- Ah, the unique and unpredictable circadian rhythms of the workaholic.
- I wasn't sleeping. I was trying to pick up a contact lens without my hands.
- Amen.

Huh?

- As of tomorrow, employees will only be able to access the building using individual security cards. Pictures will be taken next Wednesday, and employees will receive their cards in two weeks.
- What I need is a list of specific unknown problems we will encounter.
- Email is not to be used to pass on information or data. It should be used only for company business.
- This project is so important that we can't let things more important interfere.
- Doing it right is no excuse for not meeting the schedule. No one will believe you solved this problem in one day! We've been working on it for months. Now go act busy for a few weeks, and I'll let you know when it's time to tell them.
- Quote from the boss: "Teamwork is a lot of people doing what I say."
- My sister passed away, and her funeral was scheduled for Monday. When I told my boss, he said she died so that I would have to miss work on the busiest day of the year. He then asked if we could change her burial to Friday. He said, "That would be better for me."
- "We know that communication is a problem, but the company is not going to discuss it with the employees."
- We recently received a memo from senior management, saying, "This is to inform you that a memo will be issued today regarding the subject mentioned above."

- One day, my boss asked me to submit a status report to him concerning a project I was working on. I asked him if tomorrow would be soon enough. He said, "If I wanted it tomorrow, I would have waited until tomorrow to ask for it!"

You know you are drinking too much coffee when...

- You answer the door before people knock.
- You ski uphill.
- You grind your coffee beans in your mouth.
- You haven't blinked since the last lunar eclipse.
- You're the employee of the month at the local coffeehouse, and you don't even work there.
- Your eyes stay open when you sneeze.
- You chew on other people's fingernails.
- You can type sixty words per minute…with your feet.
- You don't need a hammer to pound nails.
- Your only source of nutrition comes from Splenda.
- You don't sweat, you percolate.
- You've worn out the handle on your favorite mug.
- You go to AA meetings just for the free coffee.
- You walk twenty miles on your treadmill before you realize it's not plugged in.
- You forget to unwrap candy bars before eating them.
- You've built a miniature city out of little plastic stirrers.
- People get dizzy just watching you.
- Instant coffee takes too long.
- Your birthday is a national holiday in Brazil.
- When someone says, "How are you?" you say, "Good to the last drop."
- You want to be cremated just so you can spend the rest of eternity in a coffee can.
- You're offended when people use the word "brew" to mean beer.
- You can thread a sewing machine while it's running.
- You can outlast the Energizer bunny.

- You short out motion detectors.
- You don't even wait for the water to boil anymore.
- You think being called a "drip" is a compliment.
- You don't tan; you roast.
- You help your dog chase its tail.

So you want the day off?

Let's take a look at what you are asking for.

There are 365 days per year available for work. There are 52 weeks per year that you already have 2 days off per week, leaving 261 days available for work.

Since you spend sixteen hours each day away from work, you have used up 170 days, leaving only 91 days available.

You spend thirty minutes each day on a coffee break. This accounts for twenty-three days each year, leaving only sixty-eight days available.

With a one-hour lunch period each day, you have used up another forty-eight days, leaving only twenty days available.

You normally spend two days per year on sick leave. This leaves you only eighteen days available for work.

We offer five holidays per year, so your available working time is down to thirteen days.

We generously give you twelve days' vacation per year, which leaves you only one day available for work.

And there's no way you're going to take that day off!

Get to work!

For a couple of years, I've been tired. I've been blaming it on lack of sleep and too much pressure from my job, but now I found out the real reason: I'm tired because I'm overworked.

The population of this country is 237 million. About 104 million are retired. That leaves 133 million to do the work.

There are 85 million in school, which leaves 48 million to do the work.

Of this, there are 29 million employed by the federal government, leaving 19 million to do the work.

There are 2.8 million in the Armed Forces, which leaves 16.2 million to do the work.

Take from the total the 14,800,000 people who work for state and city governments, and that leaves 1.4 million to do the work.

At any given time, there are 188,000 people in hospitals, leaving 1,212,000 to do the work.

Now, there are 1,211,998 people in prisons. That leaves just two people to do the work—you and me.

And you're sitting here reading this book!

Office pranks for the insane

- Get everyone but your target in on it, and never come by their office twice in a row wearing the same clothes.
- Staple every unimportant paper on their desk together.
- If your target has a computer, reposition the monitor every day.
- Put a live lobster or any other creature in the file cabinet.
- If the computer has speakers, turn the volume all the way up or way down depending on your mood.
- Taping down the switch hook buttons on the phone gets some interesting reactions. When the mark answers, the phone keeps ringing.
- Program the mark's phone to forward to the office paging system.
- Ask your mark, "are you getting fired? Well, that's the rumor."
- Does your coworker have fish in the office? Take the fish and leave a ransom note.
- Pull the labeled buttons off of their phone, rearrange the order, and put them back on their phone. They won't be sure of which line is which or which connects them to the boss!

- Tape your victim's telephone receiver down at the top and bottom when they are away from their desk. When they come back, call them from your desk and watch them struggle to answer.
- Put transparent tape over the readout of a calculator. It makes the numbers blurry.
- If your boss wins a prestigious award, manufacture a phony memo from the company president announcing the discontinuance of the award.
- Buy a package of approximately two hundred of those little paper bathroom cups and neatly arrange them all over the subject's desk. Then staple them all together and fill them with water. See how long it takes them to figure out how to get rid of this setup without spilling water all over their paperwork, files, computer, etc.
- Take the paper out of the copier and write, "Everything written on the flip side of this paper is a lie!" Put it back into the copier mixed with regular sheets.
- Buy a voice changer at a toy store and answer the phone in strange voices.
- At lunch, swap the worker's real food with look-a-like dog toys.
- If someone is applying for a job, call them back and leave the wrong number. They go crazy for a while until you call them back apologizing.
- If the center drawer to the victim's desk has a board under it, you can take the drawer out, take the contents out, and put the drawer back in but UPSIDE-DOWN! Then while the upside-down drawer is partially opened, put the contents back in and close it. When the unsuspecting victim opens the drawer, all the contents fall out!
- Take some cellophane and open up the glue bottle. Put the cellophane across the opening, then close the bottle. Watch the victim try to squeeze the glue out. They either open it up to check, or they squeeze too hard, breaking the cellophane and getting glue everywhere.

COMPUTER MANUAL OF A DIFFERENT SORT

Technology for countryfolk

Log on	Made a wood stove hotter.
Log off	Don't add no more wood.
Monitor	Keepin' an eye on the wood stove.
Download	Gettin' the farwood off the truck.
Ram	That thar thing what splits the farwood.
Hard drive	Gettin' home in the wintertime.
Prompt	What the mail ain't in the wintertime.
Windows	What to shut when it's cold outside.
Screen	What to shut when it's black fly season.
Byte	What them dang flys do.
Modem	Whatcha did to the hay fields.
Dot matrix	Old Dan Matrixes's wife.
Lap top	Whar the kitty sleeps.
Keyboard	Whar ya hang the dang keys.
Software	Them dang plastic forks and knives.
Mouse	What eats the grain in the barn.
Mainframe	Holds up the dang roof
Port	Fancy flatlander wine.
Enter	Northerner talk fer "C'mon in y'all."
Random access memory	When ya cain't member what ya paid fer the rifle when yore wife asks.

Computer reasoning?

Top 5 reasons why computers must be FEMALE

1. No one but their creator understands their internal logic.
2. Even the smallest mistakes are immediately committed to memory for future reference.
3. The native language used to communicate with other computers is incomprehensible to everyone else.

4. The message "Bad command or filename" is about as informative as "If you don't know why I'm mad at you, then I'm certainly not going to tell you."
5. As soon as you make a commitment to one, you find yourself spending half or more of your paycheck on accessories for it.

*****

Top 5 reasons why computers must be MALE

1. They're heavily dependent on external tools and equipment.
2. They periodically cut you off right when you think you've established a network connection.
3. They'll usually do what you ask them to do, but they won't do more than they have to, and they won't think of it on their own.
4. The lights are on, but nobody's home.
5. They look nice and shiny until you bring them home.

CHAPTER 4

On a Religious Note

Wake-up prayer

Dear Lord,

So far today, God, I've done all right. I haven't gossiped, haven't lost my temper, haven't been greedy, grumpy, nasty, selfish, or indulgent. I'm really glad about that.
But in a few minutes, Lord, I'm going to get out of bed, and from then on, I'm probably going to need a lot more help.

Thank You,
In Jesus's name, amen

Thank you, Lord

Even Though…

I clutch my blanket and growl when the alarm rings. Thank you, Lord, that I can hear.
There are many deaf.
I keep my eyes closed against the morning light as long as possible. Thank you, Lord, that I can see.
Many are blind.

I huddle in my bed and put off rising. Thank you Lord, I have the strength to rise.
There are many bedridden.
The first hour of my day is hectic. When socks are lost, toast is burned, tempers are short, and my children are so loud—thank you, Lord, for my family.
There are many lonely.
Our breakfast table never looks like the pictures in magazines, and the menu is at times unbalanced. Thank you, Lord, for the food we have.
There are many hungry.
The routine of my job often is monotonous. Thank you, Lord, for the opportunity to work.
There are many without jobs.
I grumble and bemoan my fate from day to day and wish my circumstances were not so modest.
Thank you, Lord, for life.

Prayers of the stress impaired

1. Lord, help me to relax about insignificant details beginning tomorrow at 7:41:23 a.m. EST.
2. God, help me to consider people's feelings, even if most of them are hypersensitive.
3. God, help me to take responsibility for my own actions, even though they're usually NOT my fault.
4. God, help me not to try to run everything. But if You need some help, please feel free to ask me!
5. Help me to be more laid back and help me to do it EXACTLY right.
6. God, help me to take things more seriously, especially laughter, parties, and dancing.
7. Give me patience, and I mean right NOW!
8. Lord, help me not be a perfectionist. (Did I spell that correctly?)
9. God, help me to finish everything I sta—

10. God, help me to keep my mind on one th—look, a bird!—ing at a time.
11. God, help me to do only what I can, and trust you for the rest. And would you mind putting that in writing?
12. Lord, keep me open to others' ideas, WRONG though they may be.
13. Help me be less independent, but let me do it my way.
14. Lord, help me follow established procedures today. On second thought, I'll settle for a few minutes.
15. Lord, help me slow down and notrushthroughwhatIdo.

Dear God

(Letters children sent to God as found on email.)

Dear GOD,

Instead of letting people die and having to make new ones, why don't you just keep the ones You have?

Jane

Dear GOD,

Maybe Cain and Abel would not kill each other so much if they had their own rooms. It works with my brother.

Larry

Dear GOD,

If You watch me in church on Sunday, I'll show You my new shoes.

Mickey

Dear God,

I bet it is very hard for You to love everybody in the whole world. There are only four people in our family, and I can never do it.

> Nan

Dear God,

In school, they told us what You do. Who does it when You are on vacation?

> Jane

Dear God,

I read the Bible. What does "begat" mean? Nobody will tell me.

> Love,
> Alison

Dear God,

Are You really invisible, or is it just a trick?

> Lucy

Dear God,

Is it true my father won't get into heaven if he uses his bowling words in the house?

> Anita

Dear God,

Did You mean for the giraffe to look like that, or was it an accident?

                                                           Norma

Dear God,

Who draws the lines around the countries?

                                                           Nan

Dear God,

I went to this wedding, and they kissed right in church. Is that okay?

                                                          Neil

Dear God,

What does it mean You are a jealous God? I thought You had everything.

                                                           Jane

Dear God,

Did You really mean "do unto others as they do unto you?" Because if You did, then I'm going to fix my brother.

                                                          Darla

Dear God,

Thank you for the baby brother, but what I prayed for was a PUPPY.

>Joyce

Dear God,

It rained for our whole vacation, and my father is mad! He said some things about You that people are not supposed to say, but I hope You will not hurt him anyway.

>Your friend,
>(I am not going to tell You who I am)

Dear God,

Why is Sunday school on Sunday? I thought it was supposed to be our day of rest.

>Tom L.

Dear God,

Please send me a pony. I never asked for anything before. You can look it up.

>Bruce

Dear God,

If we come back as something, please don't let me be Jennifer H. because I hate her.

>Denise

COMPUTER MANUAL OF A DIFFERENT SORT

Dear God,

If you give me a genie, like Aladdin, I will give You anything You want, except my money or my chess set.

                                                                  Raphael

Dear God,

My brother is a rat. You should give him a tail. Haha.

                                                                   Danny

Dear God,

I want to be just like my Daddy when I get big but not with so much hair all over.

                                                                     Sam

Dear God,

You don't have to worry about me. I always look both ways.

                                                                   Dean

Dear God,

I think the stapler is one of your greatest inventions.

                                                                  Ruth M.

Dear God,

   I think about You sometimes even when I'm not praying.

Elliott

Dear God,

   Of all the people who work for You, I like Noah and David the best.

Rob

Dear God,

   My brother told me about being born, but it doesn't sound right. They're just kidding, aren't they?

Marsha

Dear God,

   I would like to live 900 years like the guy in the Bible.

Love, Chris

Dear God,

   We read Thomas Edison made light. But in Sunday school, they said You did it. So I bet he stole your idea.

Sincerely,
Donna

COMPUTER MANUAL OF A DIFFERENT SORT

Dear GOD,

The bad people laughed at Noah: "You made an ark on dry land, you fool." But he was smart. He stuck with You. That's what I would do.

Eddie

Dear GOD,

I do not think anybody could be a better GOD. Well, I just want You to know, but I am not just saying that because You are GOD already.

Charles

Dear GOD,

I didn't think orange went with purple until I saw the sunset You made on Tuesday. That was cool.

Paul S.

16 books of the Bible

See if you can find sixteen of the books of the Bible in the following paragraph:

I once made a remark about the hidden books of the Bible. It was a lulu. Kept people looking so hard for the facts, and for others, it was a revelation. Some were in a jam, especially since the names of the books were not capitalized. But the truth finally struck home to numbers of readers. To others, it was a real job. We want it to be a most fascinating few moments for you. Yes, there will be some really easy ones to spot. Others may require judges to help them. I will quickly admit it usually takes an expert to find one of them, and there will be lamentations when it is found. A little lady says she brews a cup of tea so she can concentrate better. See how well you can compete. Relax, now, for there really are sixteen names of books of the Bible in this paragraph.

(ANSWER: *Mark, Luke, Kings, Acts, Revelation, James, Ruth, Numbers, Job, Amos, Esther, Judges, Titus, Lamentations, Hebrews,* and *Peter*)

Kids 'n' religion

A mother took her three-year-old daughter to church for the first time. The church lights were lowered, and then the choir came down the aisle, carrying lighted candles. All was quiet until the little one started to sing in a loud voice, "Happy Birthday to you, happy birthday to you…"

*****

Nine-year-old Joey was asked by his mother what he had learned in Sunday school.

"Well, Mom, our teacher told us how God sent Moses behind enemy lines on a rescue mission to lead the Israelites out of Egypt. When he got to the Red Sea, he had his engineers build a pontoon bridge, and all the people walked across safely. Then he used his walkie-talkie to radio headquarters for reinforcements. They sent bombers to blow up the bridge, and all the Israelites were saved."

"Now, Joey, is that really what your teacher taught you?" his mom asked.

"Well, no, but if I told it the way the teacher did, you'd never believe it!"

*****

A child came home from Sunday school and told his mother that he had learned a new song about a cross-eyed bear named "Gladly." It took his mother a while before she realized that the hymn was really "Gladly, the Cross I'd Bear."

*****

One summer evening, during a violent thunderstorm, a mother was tucking her small boy into bed. She was about to turn off the light when he asked with a tremor in his voice, "Mommy, will you sleep with me tonight?"
The mother smiled and gave him a reassuring hug.
"I can't, dear," she said. "I have to sleep in Daddy's room."
A long silence was broken at last by his shaking little voice: "The big sissy."

Hymns

Dentist Hymn	"Crown Him with Many Crowns"
Weatherman Hymn	"There Shall Be Showers of Blessings"
Contractor Hymn	"The Church's One Foundation"
Tailor Hymn	"Holy, Holy, Holy"
Golfer Hymn	"There's a Green Hill Far Away"
Politician Hymn	"Standing on the Promises"
Optometrist Hymn	"Open My Eyes That I Might See"
IRS Agent Hymn	"I Surrender All"
Gossip Hymn	"Pass It On"
Electrician Hymn	"Send the Light"
Shopper Hymn	"Sweet By and By"
Realtor Hymn	"I've Got a Mansion, Just Over the Hilltop"
Massage Therapist Hymn	"He Touched Me"
Doctor Hymn	"The Great Physician"

For those who speed on the highway…

Forty-five miles per hour	"God Will Take Care of You"
Fifty-five miles per hour	"Guide Me, O Thou Great Jehovah"
Sixty-five miles per hour	"Nearer My God to Thee"
Seventy-five miles per hour	"Nearer Still Nearer"
Eighty-five miles per hour	"This World Is Not My Home"
Ninety-five miles per hour	"Lord, I'm Coming Home"
and over one hundred miles per hour	"Precious Memories"

Letters to pastors

Dear Pastor,

 I know God loves everybody, but He never met my sister.

Yours sincerely,
Arnold
Age eight

Dear Pastor,

 Please say in your sermon that Peter P. has been a good boy all week. I am Peter P.

Sincerely,
Pete
Age nine

COMPUTER MANUAL OF A DIFFERENT SORT

Dear Pastor,

My father should be a minister. Every day, he gives us a sermon about something.

Robert A.,
Age eleven

Dear Pastor,

I'm sorry I can't leave more money in the offering plate, but my father didn't give me a raise in my allowance. Could you have a sermon about a raise in my allowance?

Love,
Patty
Age ten

Dear Pastor,

My mother is very religious. She goes to play bingo at church every week, even if she has a cold.

Yours truly,
Annette
Age nine

Dear Pastor,

I would like to go to heaven someday because I know my brother won't be there.

Stephen
Age eight

Dear Pastor,

    I think a lot more people would come to your church if you moved it to Disneyland.

> Loreen
> Age nine

Dear Pastor,

    I liked your sermon where you said that good health is more important than money, but I still want a raise in my allowance.

> Sincerely,
> Eleanor
> Age twelve

Dear Pastor,

    Please pray for all the airline pilots. I am flying to California tomorrow.

> Laurie
> Age ten

Dear Pastor,

    I hope to go to heaven someday, but later than sooner.

> Love,
> Ellen
> Age nine

COMPUTER MANUAL OF A DIFFERENT SORT

Dear Pastor,

Please say a prayer for our Little League team. We need God's help or a new pitcher. Thank you.

Alexander
Age ten

Dear Pastor,

My father says I should learn the Ten Commandments. But I don't think I want to because we have enough rules already in my house.

Joshua
Age ten

Dear Pastor,

Who does God pray to? Is there a God for God?

Sincerely,
Christopher
Age nine

Dear Pastor,

Are there any devils on earth? I think there may be one in my class.

Carla
Age ten

Dear Pastor,

I liked your sermon on Sunday, especially when it was finished.

Ralph
Age eleven

Dear Pastor,

How does God know the good people from the bad people? Do you tell Him, or does He read about it in the newspapers?

Sincerely,
Marie
Age nine

Good instructions

- Be Fishers of Men… You catch 'em, He'll clean 'em.
- A family altar can alter a family.
- A lot of kneeling will keep you in good standing.
- Don't put a question mark where God put a full stop.
- Don't wait for six strong men to take you to church.
- Exercise daily. Walk with the Lord!
- Forbidden fruits create many jams.
- Give God what's right, not what's left!
- Give Satan an inch, and he'll be a ruler.
- God doesn't call the qualified. He qualifies the called.
- God grades on the cross, not the curve.
- God loves everyone but probably prefers "fruits of the spirit" over "religious nuts."
- God promises a safe landing, not a calm passage.
- Having truth decay? Brush up on your Bible!
- He who angers you controls you!
- He who is good at making excuses is seldom good for anything else.

COMPUTER MANUAL OF A DIFFERENT SORT

- He who kneels before God can stand before anyone!
- Kindness is difficult to give away because it keeps coming back.
- Most people want to serve God but only in an advisory capacity.
- Never give the devil a ride! He will always want to drive!
- Nothing ruins the truth like stretching it.
- "Pray" is a four-letter word that you can say anywhere.
- Prayer: Don't give God instructions—just report for duty!
- The Will of God will never take you to where the Grace of God will not protect you.
- This church is "Prayer Conditioned"!
- To be almost saved is to be totally lost.
- WARNING: Exposure to the Son may prevent burning!
- Watch your step carefully! Everyone else does!
- We don't change the message; the message changes us.
- We set the sail; God makes the wind.
- Wisdom has two parts: Having a lot to say AND not saying it.
- Worry is the darkroom in which "negatives" are developed.

Bible questions

Q. Who was the greatest financier in the Bible?
A. Noah—he was floating his stock while everyone else was in liquidation.

Q. Who was the greatest female financier in the Bible?
A. Pharoah's daughter—she went down to the bank of the Nile and drew out a little prophet.

Q. What kind of man was Boaz before he got married?
A. Ruth-less.

Q. Who was the first drug addict in the Bible?
A. Nebuchadnezzar—he was on grass for seven years.

Q. What kind of motor vehicles are in the Bible?
A. Jehovah drove Adam and Eve out of the Garden in a Fury.
David's Triumph was heard throughout the land.
Honda…because the apostles were all in one Accord.
Second Corinthians 4:8 describes going out in service in a Volkswagen Beetle: "We are pressed in every way but not cramped beyond movement."

Q. Who was the greatest comedian in the Bible?
A. Samson—he brought the house down.

Q. Where is the first baseball game in the Bible?
A. In the big inning, Eve stole first, and Adam stole second. Cain struck out Abel, and the Prodigal Son came home. The Giants and the Angels were rained out.

Q. How did Adam and Eve feel when expelled from the garden of Eden?
A. They were really put out.

Q. What is one of the first things that Adam and Eve did after they were kicked out?
A. They raised Cain.

Q. What excuse did Adam give to his children as to why he no longer lived in Eden?
A. Your mother ate us out of the house and home.

Q. The ark was built in three stories, and the top story had a window to let light in, but how did they get light to the bottom two stories?
A. They used floodlights.

Q. Who is the greatest babysitter mentioned in the Bible?
A. David—he rocked Goliath to sleep.

COMPUTER MANUAL OF A DIFFERENT SORT

Q. Why was Goliath so surprised when David hit him with a slingshot?
A. The thought had never entered his head before.

Q. If Goliath is resurrected, would you like to tell him the joke about David and Goliath?
A. No, he already fell for it once.

Q. What do they call pastors in Germany?
A. German Shepherds.

Q. What is the best way to get to Paradise?
A. Turn right and go straight.

Q. Which servant of Jehovah was the most flagrant lawbreaker in the Bible?
A. Moses, because he broke all Ten Commandments at once.

Q. Which area of Palestine was especially wealthy?
A. The area around the Jordan—the banks were always overflowing.

Q. How do we know that Job went to a chiropractor?
A. Because in Job 16:12, we read, "I had come to be at ease, but he proceeded to shake me up: and he grabbed me by the back of the neck and proceeded to smash me."

Q. Where is the first tennis match mentioned in the Bible?
A. When Joseph served in Pharaoh's court.

Q: Which Bible character had no parents?
A: Joshua, son of Nun.

Q: Why didn't Noah go fishing?
A: He only had two worms!

Q: How do we know that they played cards in the ark?
A: Because Noah sat on the deck.

Christian flying

There was this Christian lady who had to do a lot of traveling for her business, so she did a lot of flying. But flying made her nervous, so she always took her Bible along with her to read and it helped relax her.

One time, she was sitting next to a man. When he saw her pull out her Bible, he gave a little chuckle and went back to what he was doing. After a while, he turned to her and asked, "You don't really believe all that stuff in there, do you?"

The lady replied, "Of course I do—it is the Bible."

He said, "Well, what about that guy that was swallowed by that whale?"

She replied, "Oh, Jonah. Yes, I believe that—it's in the Bible."

He asked, "Well, how do you suppose he survived all that time inside the whale?"

The lady said, "Well, I don't really know—I guess when I get to heaven, I will ask him."

"What if he isn't in heaven?" the man asked sarcastically.

"Then you can ask him," replied the lady.

Bulletin bloopers!

- Bertha Belch, a missionary from Africa, will be speaking tonight at Calvary Memorial Church in Racine. Come tonight and hear Bertha Belch all the way from Africa.
- Announcement in the church bulletin for a National Prayer and Fasting conference: "The cost for attending the Fasting and Prayer conference includes meals."
- Our youth basketball team is back in action on Wednesday at 8:00 p.m. in the recreation hall. Come out and watch us kill Christ the King.

COMPUTER MANUAL OF A DIFFERENT SORT

- "Ladies, don't forget the rummage sale. It's a chance to get rid of those things not worth keeping around the house. Don't forget your husbands."
- Next Sunday is the family hayride and bonfire at the Fowlers'. Bring your own hot dogs and guns. Friends are welcome! Everyone, come for a fun time.
- The peacemaking meeting scheduled for today has been canceled due to a conflict.
- The sermon this morning is "Jesus Walks on the Water." The sermon for tonight is "Searching for Jesus."
- Next Thursday, there will be tryouts for the choir. They need all the help they can get.
- Barbara remains in the hospital and needs blood donors for more transfusions. She is also having trouble sleeping and requests tapes of Pastor Jack's sermons.
- Remember in prayer the many who are sick of our community. Smile at someone who is hard to love. Say "hell" to someone who doesn't care much about you.
- Irving Benson and Jessie Carter were married on October 24 in the church. So ends a friendship that began in their school days.
- Please place your donation in the envelope along with the deceased person(s) you want to be remembered.
- Attend, and you will hear an excellent speaker and heave a healthy lunch.
- The church will host an evening of fine dining, superb entertainment, and gracious hostility.
- The Scouts are saving aluminum cans, bottles, and other items to be recycled. Proceeds will be used to cripple children.
- Ladies Bible Study will be held Thursday morning at ten. All ladies are invited to lunch in the Fellowship Hall after the BS is done.
- The pastor would appreciate it if the ladies of the congregation would lend him their electric girdles for the pancake breakfast next Sunday morning.

- Low Self Esteem Support Group will meet on Thursday at 7:00 p.m. Please use the back door.
- The pastor will preach his farewell message, after which the choir will sing "Break Forth into Joy."
- A songfest was hell at the Methodist church on Wednesday.
- The eighth-graders will be presenting Shakespeare's Hamlet in the church basement on Friday at 7:00 p.m. The Congregation is invited to attend this tragedy.
- Thursday night Potluck Supper. Prayer and medication to follow.
- Mrs. Johnson will be entering the hospital this week for testes.
- Please join us as we show our support for Amy and Alan, who are preparing for the girth of their first child.
- Our next song is "Angels We Have Heard Get High."
- Don't let worry kill you. Let the church help.
- For those of you who have children and don't know it, we have a nursery downstairs.
- The service will close with Little Drops of Water. One of the ladies will start quietly, and the rest of the congregation will join in.
- Eight new choir robes are currently needed due to the addition of several new members and to the deterioration of some older ones.
- Remember in prayer the many who are sick of our church and community.
- The rosebud on the altar this morning is to announce the birth of David Alan B, the sin of Rev. and Mrs. Julius B.
- This afternoon there will be a meeting in the South and North ends of the church. Children will be baptized at both ends.
- Wednesday, the ladies' Liturgy Society will meet. Mrs. Jones will sing "Put Me in My Little Bed," accompanied by the pastor.

- Thursday at 5:00 p.m., there will be a meeting of the Little Mother Club. All wishing to become little mothers, please see the minister in his study.
- This being Easter Sunday, we will ask Mrs. Lewis to come forward and lay an egg on the altar.
- Next Sunday, a special collection will be taken to defray the cost of the new carpet. All those wishing to do something on the new carpet will come forward and do so.
- The ladies of the church have cast off clothing of every kind, and they may be seen in the church basement on Friday.
- A bean supper will be held on Tuesday evening in the church hall. Music will follow.
- At the evening service tonight, the sermon topic will be "What is Hell?" Come early and listen to our choir practice.
- The dieting class will meet at 7:00 p.m. at the First Presbyterian Church. Please use a large double door at the side entrance.
- Pastor is on vacation. Massages can be given to the secretary.
- The senior choir invites any member of the congregation who enjoys sinning to join the choir.
- The associate pastor unveiled the church's new tithing campaign slogan last Sunday: "I upped my pledge—up yours."

The preacher and the song leader

There was a church where the preacher and the song leader were not getting along. This began to spill over into the worship service. One week, the preacher preached on commitment and dedicating ourselves to service. The song leader then led the song "I Shall Not Be Moved."

The next Sunday, the preacher preached on giving and giving gladly to the work of the Lord. The song leader then led the song "Jesus Paid It All."

The next Sunday, the preacher preached on gossiping and how we should watch our tongues. The song leader then led the song "I Love to Tell the Story."

The preacher became very disgusted over the situation. The next Sunday, he told the congregation he was considering resigning. The leader then led the song "Oh, Why Not Tonight."

As it came to pass, the preacher resigned and the next week informed the church that it was Jesus that led him there, and it was Jesus that was taking him away. The song leader then led the song "What a Friend We Have in Jesus."

CHAPTER 5

Something to Think About

Ethical questions

Question 1:

If you knew a woman who was pregnant, who had eight kids already—three who were deaf, two who were blind, and one mentally retarded—and she had syphilis, would you recommend that she have an abortion? *Read the next question before reading the answer to this one.*

Question 2:

It is time to elect the world leader and your vote counts. Here are the facts about the three leading candidates.

Candidate A

Associates with crooked politicians and consults astrologists. He's had two mistresses. He also chain smokes and drinks eight to ten martinis a day.

Candidate B

He was kicked out of office twice, sleeps until noon, used opium in college, and drinks a quart of whisky every evening.

Candidate C

He is a decorated war hero. He's a vegetarian, doesn't smoke, drinks an occasional beer, and hasn't had any extramarital affairs.

Which of these candidates would be your choice? *Decide first, then check the answer.*

*****

Candidate A is Franklin D. Roosevelt
Candidate B is Winston Churchill
Candidate C is Adolph Hitler

By the way…if you answered yes to the abortion question, you would have killed Beethoven.

—*Author unknown*

Isn't it funny…

How $10 looks so big when we take it to church and so small when we take it to the store?

How big sixty minutes are when serving God, but how small when we are fishing, or playing golf or basketball?

How laborious it is to read a chapter in the Bible, but how easy to read two hundred to three hundred pages of a novel?

How we believe what a person or newspaper says but question what the Bible says?

How we can't think of anything to say when we pray but don't have any trouble gossiping about someone?

How we need two or three weeks to fit a church event into our schedule but have no problem adjusting for a social event at the last minute.

How we get thrilled when a football game goes into extra overtime but complain when a sermon is longer than we expected?

How people scramble to get a front seat at a game but scramble to get a back seat at church?

How difficult it is to share the gospel with others, but how simple it is to just sit and talk about the game?

How everyone wants to go to heaven, provided they don't have to believe…think…say…or do anything?

Funny, isn't it—or is it?

—*Author unknown*

Keep your fork!

There was a woman who had been diagnosed with a terminal illness and was given three months to live. As she began getting her things "in order," she called her pastor and asked him to come to her house to discuss certain aspects of her final wishes. She told him which songs she wanted sung at the service, what scriptures she wanted read, and in what dress she wanted to be buried. She also requested to be buried with her favorite Bible in her left hand.

Everything was in order, and as the pastor was preparing to leave, the woman suddenly remembered one final request that was very important to her.

"Please, Pastor, just one more thing," she said excitedly.

"Sure, what is it?" came the pastor's reply.

"This is very important to me," the woman continued.

"I want to be buried holding a fork in my right hand."

The pastor gazed at the woman, at a loss for words.

"That surprises you, doesn't it?" the woman asked.

The pastor replied, "Well, to be quite honest, I'm puzzled by the request." The woman explained. "You see, Pastor, in all my years of attending church socials and potluck dinners, I remember that when the dishes were being cleared after the main course, someone would inevitably lean over to me and say, "Keep your fork." It was my favorite part because I knew that something better was coming, like velvety chocolate cake or deep-dish apple pie. Something wonderful and with substance to end the great meal."

The pastor listened intently, and a smile came upon his face.

The woman continued, "So I just want people to see me there in the casket with a fork in my hand, and I want them to wonder, 'What's with the fork?' Then I want you to tell them 'Keep your fork... The best is yet to come.'"

The pastor's eyes welled up with tears of joy as he hugged the woman goodbye. He knew that this would be one of the last times that he would see her before her death. But he also knew that the woman had a better grasp of Heaven than he did. She *knew* and trusted that the best was yet to come.

At the funeral, everyone who walked by the woman's casket saw her wearing a beautiful dress with her favorite Bible held in her left hand and a fork held in her right hand. Over and over, the pastor heard people ask the question, "Why is she holding a fork?" and his smile began to get larger and brighter each time.

During his message, the pastor told the people about the conversation that he had with the woman shortly before she died. He explained the fork and what it symbolized to her. The pastor told everyone how he could not stop thinking about the fork and how he hoped that they would not be able to stop thinking about it either. That fork, and the meaning of it to the woman, had quite an impact on everyone, and they are still sharing the story with people they meet.

And now it has been shared with you. So the next time you reach for your fork, let it remind you, oh so gently, that the best is yet to come!

—Author unknown

The four stages of life…

1. You believe in Santa Claus.
2. You don't believe in Santa Claus.
3. You are Santa Claus.
4. You look like Santa Claus.

The paradox of our time

The paradox of our time in history is that we have taller buildings but shorter tempers; wider freeways but narrower viewpoints; spend more but have less; buy more but enjoy it less.

We have bigger houses and smaller families; more conveniences but less time; we have more degrees but less sense; more knowledge but less judgment; more experts but more problems; more medicine but less wellness.

We drink too much, smoke too much, spend too recklessly, laugh too little, drive too fast, get too angry too quickly, stay up too late, get up too tired, read too seldom, watch TV too much, and pray too seldom.

We have multiplied our possessions but reduced our values. We talk too much, love too seldom, and hate too often. We've learned how to make a living but not a life; we've added years to life, not life to years.

We've been to the moon and back but have trouble crossing the street to meet the new neighbor. We've conquered outer space, but not inner space. We've done larger things, but not better things. We've cleaned up the air but polluted the soul.

We've split the atom, but not our prejudice. We write more but learn less; we plan more but accomplish less. We've learned to rush but not to wait.

We have higher incomes but lower morals; more food but less appeasement; build more computers to hold more information to produce more copies than ever but have less communication. We've become long on quantity but short on quality.

These are the times of fast foods and slow digestion, tall men and short character, steep profits and shallow relationships.

These are the times of world peace but domestic warfare; more leisure but less fun; more kinds of food but less nutrition.

These are days of two incomes but more divorce; fancier houses but broken homes.

These are days of quick trips, disposable diapers, throwaway morality, one-night stands, overweight bodies, and pills that do everything from cheer, to quiet, to kill.

It is a time when there is much in the show window and nothing in the stockroom—a time when technology can bring this letter to you via email, and a time when you can choose either to make a difference or to just hit delete…

—Author unknown

Positive attitude

Read this and let it really sink in. Then choose how you start your day tomorrow.

Michael is the kind of guy you love to hate. He is always in a good mood and always has something positive to say. When someone would ask him how he was doing, he would reply, "If I were any better, I would be twins."

He was a natural motivator. If an employee was having a bad day, Michael was telling the employee how to look on the positive side of the situation.

Seeing this style really made me curious, so one day, I went up to Michael and asked him, "I don't get it! You can't be a positive person all of the time. How do you do it?"

Michael replied, "Each morning, I wake up and say to myself, 'Mike, you have two choices today. You can choose to be in a good mood, or you can choose to be in a bad mood.' I choose to be in a good mood. Each time something bad happens, I can choose to be a victim, or I can choose to learn from it. I choose to learn from it. Every time someone comes to me complaining, I can choose to accept their complaining, or I can point out the positive side of life. I choose the positive side of life."

"Yeah, right, it isn't that easy," I protested.

"Yes, it is," Michael said. "Life is all about choices. When you cut away all the junk, every situation is a choice. You choose how you react to situations. You choose how people will affect your mood. You choose to be in a good mood or a bad mood. The bottom line is, it's your choice how you live life."

I reflected on what Michael said. Soon thereafter, I left the tower industry to start my own business. We lost touch, but I often thought about him when I made a choice about life instead of reacting. Several years later, I heard that Michael was involved in a serious accident, falling some sixty feet from a communications tower. After eighteen hours of surgery and weeks of intensive care, Michael was released from the hospital with rods placed in his back.

I saw Michael about six months after the accident. When I asked him how he was, he replied. "If I were any better, I'd be twins. Wanna see my scars?" I declined to see his wounds but did ask him what had gone through his mind as the accident took place.

"The first thing that went through my mind was the well-being of my soon-to-be-born daughter," Michael replied. "Then as I lay on the ground, I remembered that I had two choices: I could choose to live, or I could choose to die. I chose to live."

"Weren't you scared? Did you lose consciousness?" I asked.

Michael continued, "The paramedics were great. They kept telling me I was going to be fine. But when they wheeled me into the ER, and I saw the expressions on the faces of the doctors and nurses, I got really scared. In their eyes, I read, 'He's a dead man.' I knew I needed to take action."

"What did you do?" I asked.

"Well, there was a big, burly nurse shouting questions at me," said Michael. "She asked if I was allergic to anything. 'Yes,' I replied. The doctors and nurses stopped working as they waited for my reply. I took a deep breath and yelled, 'Gravity.' Over their laughter, I told them, 'I am choosing to live.' Operate on me as if I am alive, not dead.'"

Michael lived, thanks to the skill of his doctors but also because of his amazing attitude. I learned from him that every day we have the choice to live fully. Attitude, after all, is everything.

—Author unknown

Rare works of art

A wealthy man and his son loved to collect rare works of art. They had everything in their collection, from Picasso to Raphael. They would often sit together and admire the great works of art.

When the Vietnam conflict broke out, the son went to war. He was very courageous and died in battle while rescuing another soldier. The father was notified and grieved deeply for his only son. About a month later, just before Christmas, there was a knock at the door. A young man stood at the door with a large package in his hands.

He said, "Sir, you don't know me, but I am the soldier for whom your son gave his life. He saved many lives that day, and he was carrying me to safety when a bullet struck him in the heart, and he died instantly. He often talked about you and your love for art." The young man held out his package. "I know this isn't much. I'm not really a great artist, but I think your son would have wanted you to have this."

The father opened the package. It was a portrait of his son, painted by the young man. He stared in awe at the way the soldier had captured the personality of his son in the painting. The father was so drawn to the eyes that his own eyes welled up with tears. He thanked the young man and offered to pay him for the picture.

"Oh no, sir. I could never repay what your son did for me. It's a gift."

The father hung the portrait over his mantle. Every time visitors came to his home, he took them to see the portrait of his son before he showed them any of the other great works he had collected.

The man died a few months later. There was to be a great auction of his paintings. Many influential people gathered, excited over seeing the great paintings and having an opportunity to purchase one for their collection. On the platform sat the painting of the son. The auctioneer pounded his gavel. "We will start the bidding with this picture of the son. Who will bid for this picture?" There was silence.

Then a voice in the back of the room shouted, "We want to see the famous paintings. Skip this one."

But the auctioneer persisted, "Will someone bid for this painting? Who will start the bidding? $100, $200?"

Another voice shouted angrily, "We didn't come to see this painting. We came to see the Van Goghs, the Rembrandts. Get on with the real bids!" But still, the auctioneer continued, "The son! The son! Who'll take the son?" Finally, a voice came from the very back of the room. It was the longtime gardener of the man and his son. "I'll give $10 for the painting."

Being a poor man, it was all he could afford. "We have $10. Who will bid $20?"

"Give it to him for $10. Let's see the masters."

"$10 is the bid, won't someone bid $20?"

The crowd was becoming angry. They didn't want the picture of the son. They wanted more worthy investments for their collections. The auctioneer pounded the gavel.

"Going once, twice, SOLD for $10!"

A man sitting in the second row shouted, "Now let's get on with the collection!" The auctioneer laid down his gavel. "I'm sorry, the auction is over."

"What about the paintings?"

"I am sorry. When I was called to conduct this auction, I was told of a secret stipulation in the will. I was not allowed to reveal that stipulation until this time. Only the painting of the son would be auctioned. Whoever bought that painting would inherit the entire estate, including the paintings. The man who took the son gets everything!"

God gave His son two thousand years ago to die on a cruel cross. Much like the auctioneer, His message today is, "The son, the son, who'll take the son?" because, you see, whoever takes the Son gets everything.

—*Author unknown*

Things learned from children

1. A king-size waterbed holds enough water to fill a two-thousand-square-foot house four inches deep.
2. If you spray hair spray on dust bunnies and run over them with roller blades, they can ignite.
3. A 3-year-old's voice is louder than two hundred adults in a crowded restaurant.
4. If you hook a dog leash over a ceiling fan, the motor is not strong enough to rotate a forty-two-pound boy wearing Batman underwear and a Superman cape. It is strong enough, however, to spread paint on all four walls of a twenty-by-twenty-foot room.
5. You should not throw baseballs up when the ceiling fan is on. When using the ceiling fan as a bat, you have to throw the ball up a few times before you get a hit. A ceiling fan can hit a baseball a long way.
6. The glass in windows (even double pane) doesn't stop a baseball that is hit by a ceiling fan.
7. When you hear the toilet flush and then someone says "Uh-oh," it's already too late.
8. Brake fluid mixed with bleach makes smoke, and lots of it.
9. A six-year-old can start a fire with a flint rock even though a thirty-six-year-old man says they can only do it in the movies.
10. No matter how much Jell-O you put in a swimming pool, you still can't walk on water.
11. Pool filters do not like Jell-O.
12. Garbage bags do not make good parachutes.
13. Marbles in gas tanks make lots of noise when driving.
14. Always look in the oven before you turn it on. Plastic toys do not like ovens.
15. The spin cycle on the washing machine does not make earthworms dizzy. It will, however, make cats dizzy, and cats throw up twice their body weight when dizzy.

The pumpkin

A lady had recently been baptized. One of her coworkers asked her what it was like to be a Christian. She was caught off guard and didn't know how to answer, but when she looked up, she saw a jack-o-lantern on the desk and answered, "It's like being a pumpkin."

The worker asked her to explain that one. "Well, God picks you from the patch and brings you in and washes off all the dirt on the outside that you got from being around all the other pumpkins. Then he cuts off the top and takes all the yucky stuff out from inside. He removes all those seeds of doubt, hate, greed, etc. Then he carves you a new smiling face and puts his light inside you to shine for all to see."

It is our choice to either stay outside and rot on the vine or come inside and be something new and bright. You'll never look at a pumpkin the same way again.

—Author unknown

All I need to know about life I learned from a cow

1. Wake up in a happy mooo-d.
2. Don't cry over spilled milk.
3. When chewing your cud, remember, there's no fat, no calories, no cholesterol, and no taste!
4. The grass is green on the other side of the fence.
5. Turn the udder cheek and mooo-ve on.
6. Seize every opportunity and milk it for all its worth!
7. It's better to be seen and not herd.
8. Honor thy fodder and thy mother and all your udder relatives.
9. Never take any bull from anybody.
10. Always let them know who's the bossy.
11. Black and white is always an appropriate fashion statement.
12. Don't forget to cow-nt your blessings every day.

13. A farmer was milking his cow. He was just starting to get a good rhythm going when a bug flew into the barn and started circling his head. Suddenly, the bug flew into the cow's ear. The farmer didn't think much about it until the bug squirted out into his bucket. It was in one ear and out the udder.
14. A little girl was visiting her uncle, who was fixing to milk a cow. She asked her uncle how he got the milk out of the cow. The uncle proceeded to show her how he milked a cow. Then the little girl asked, "How do you get it IN there?"

Everything I need to know about life I learned from Noah's ark

1. Don't miss the boat.
2. Remember that we are all in the same boat.
3. Plan ahead. It wasn't raining when Noah built the Ark.
4. Stay fit. When you're six hundred years old, someone may ask you to do something really big.
5. Don't listen to critics; just get on with the job that needs to be done.
6. Build your future on high ground.
7. For safety's sake, travel in pairs.
8. Speed isn't always an advantage. The snails were on board with the cheetahs.
9. When you're stressed, float for a while.
10. Remember…the ark was built by amateurs, the Titanic by professionals.
11. No matter the storm, when you are with God, there's always a rainbow waiting.

Insights

- Love is blind—but marriage is an eye-opener.

- Growing old gracefully—my wife is just as beautiful as when I married her twenty years ago. Now it just takes her longer.
- Courtship—is like looking at the beautiful photos in a seed catalog.
- Marriage—is what actually comes up in your garden.
- Success—is getting what you want. Happiness—is wanting what you get.
- The length of a minute depends on which side of a bathroom door you're standing on.
- The most effective way to remember your spouse's birthday is to forget it once.
- Some people are so determined to find blissful happiness that they overlook a lifetime of contentment.
- A true music lover is a man who puts his ear to the keyhole to listen to a beautiful woman singing in the tub.
- Experience is what you get when you don't get what you want.
- The only good thing about being imperfect is the joy it brings to others.
- There are some who feel it is inappropriate to make fun of the holy institution of marriage. Then there are others who know it's the only way we can live with it.
- Our real-world dictionary defines a pessimist as an optimist with experience.
- My marriage is a continuous process of getting used to things I hadn't expected.
- Before we got married, I caught her in my arms. Now I catch her in my pockets.
- What's the difference between a vision and a sight? When my wife gets dressed up for a party, she looks like a vision—and when she wakes up in the morning, she's a sight.
- My wife only has two complaints—nothing to wear and not enough closet space.
- Bigamy is having one wife too many. Some say monogamy is the same.

- Q: Why did the polygamist cross the aisle?
  A: To get to the other bride.
- Cosmetics—a woman's means for keeping a man from reading between the lines.
- Q: What's the best way to get a youthful figure?
  A: Ask a woman her age.
- Words to live by: Do not argue with a spouse who is packing your parachute.
- Some people think life begins at conception, while others think life begins at birth. But some believe that life begins when the kid moves out, and the dog he left behind dies.

Great truths about life

From children...

1. No matter how hard you try, you can't baptize cats.
2. When your mom is mad at your dad, don't let her brush your hair.
3. If your sister hits you, don't hit her back. They always catch the second person.
4. Never ask a three-year-old to hold a tomato.
5. You can't trust dogs to watch your food.
6. Don't sneeze when someone is cutting your hair.
7. Puppies still have bad breath even after eating a Tic Tac.
8. Never hold a dustbuster and a cat at the same time.
9. School lunches stick to the wall.
10. You can't hide a piece of broccoli in a glass of milk.
11. Don't wear polka-dot underwear under white shorts.

From adults...

1. Raising teenagers is like trying to nail Jell-O to a tree.
2. There's always a lot to be thankful for if you take the time to look for it. For example, I am sitting here thinking how nice it is that wrinkles don't hurt.

3. Reason to smile: Every seven minutes of every day, someone in an aerobics class pulls a hamstring.
4. The best way to keep kids at home is to make the home a pleasant atmosphere…and let the air out of their tires.
5. Families are like fudge…mostly sweet with a few nuts.
6. Middle age is when you choose cereal for the fiber, not the toy.
7. The more you complain, the longer God lets you live.
8. If you can remain calm, you don't have all the facts.
9. Eat a live toad first thing in the morning, and nothing worse can happen to you the rest of the day.

Great truths about growing old…

1. Growing old is mandatory; growing up is optional.
2. Forget the health food. I need all the preservatives I can get.
3. When you fall down, you wonder what else you can do while you're down there.
4. You're getting old when you get the same sensation from a rocking chair that you once got from a roller coaster.
5. It's frustrating when you know all the answers, but nobody bothers to ask you the questions.
6. Time may be a great healer, but it's a lousy beautician.
7. Wisdom comes with age, but sometimes age comes alone.
8. Age is a matter of mind. If you don't mind, it doesn't matter.

Kids' instructions on life (according to email)

When you want something expensive, ask your grandparents.

Matthew
Age twelve

Never smart off to a teacher whose eyes and ears are twitching.

> Andrew
> Age nine

Wear a hat when feeding seagulls.

> Rocky
> Age nine

Sleep in your clothes so you'll be dressed in the morning.

> Stephanie
> Age eight

Don't flush the toilet when your dad's in the shower.

> Lamar
> Age ten

Never ask for anything that costs more than five dollars when your parents are doing taxes.

> Carol
> Age nine

Never bug a pregnant mom.

> Nicholas
> Age eleven

Don't ever be too full for dessert.

> Kelly
> Age ten

COMPUTER MANUAL OF A DIFFERENT SORT

When your dad is mad and asks you, "Do I look stupid?" don't answer him.

> Heather
> Age sixteen

Never tell your mom her diet's not working.

> Michael
> Age fourteen

Don't pick on your sister when she's holding a baseball bat.

> Joel
> Age twelve

When you get a bad grade in school, show it to your mom when she's on the phone.

> Alyesha
> Age thirteen

Never spit when on a roller coaster.

> Scott
> Age eleven

Never do pranks at a police station.

> Sam
> Age ten

Beware of cafeteria food when it looks like it's moving.

> Rob
> Age ten

Never tell your little brother that you're not going to do what your mom told you to do.

Hank
Age twelve

Remember you're never too old to hold your father's hand.

Molly
Age eleven

Listen to your brain. It has lots of information.

Chelsey
Age seven

Stay away from prunes.

Randy
Age nine

Never dare your little brother to paint the family car.

Phillip
Age thirteen

Forget the cake; go for the icing.

Cynthia
Age eight

Remember the two places you are always welcome—church and grandma's house.

Joanne
Age eleven

COMPUTER MANUAL OF A DIFFERENT SORT

Today is a gift

> Yesterday is history.
> Tomorrow is a mystery.
> Today is a gift.
> (That's why it's called THE PRESENT.)
>
> —Author unknown

The empty egg

Jeremy was born with a twisted body and a slow mind. At the age of twelve, he was still in second grade, seemingly unable to learn. His teacher, Ms. Miller, often became exasperated with him. He would squirm in his seat, drool, and make grunting noises. At other times, he spoke clearly and distinctly, as if a spot of light had penetrated the darkness of his brain. Most of the time, however, Jeremy just irritated his teacher.

One day, she called his parents and asked them to come in for a consultation. As his parents entered the empty classroom, Ms. Miller said to them, "Jeremy really belongs in a special school. It isn't fair to him to be with younger children who don't have learning problems. Why, there is a five-year gap between his age and that of the other students."

Jeremy's mother cried softly into a tissue while her husband spoke.

"Ms. Miller," he said, "there is no school of that kind nearby. It would be a terrible shock for Jeremy if we had to take him out of this school. We know he really likes it here."

Jeremy's teacher sat for a long time after they had left, staring at the snow outside the window. Its coldness seemed to seep into her soul. She wanted to sympathize with Jeremy's parents. After all, their only child had a terminal illness. But it wasn't fair to keep him in her class. She had eighteen other youngsters to teach, and Jeremy was a distraction. Furthermore, he would never learn to read and write. Why waste any more time trying?

As she pondered the situation, guilt washed over her. Here I am complaining when my problems are nothing compared to that poor family, she thought. Lord, please help me to be more patient with Jeremy. From that day on, she tried hard to ignore Jeremy's noises and his blank stares. Then one day, he limped to her desk, dragging his bad leg behind him.

"I love you, Ms. Miller," he exclaimed, loud enough for the whole class to hear.

The other students snickered, and Ms. Miller's face turned red. She stammered, "Wh-why, that's very nice, Jeremy. N-now please take your seat."

Spring came, and the children talked excitedly about the coming of Easter. Doris told them the story of Jesus, and then, to emphasize the idea of new life springing forth, she gave each of the children a large plastic egg.

"Now," she said to them, "I want you to take this home and bring it back tomorrow with something inside that shows new life. Do you understand?"

"Yes, Ms. Miller," the children responded enthusiastically, all except for Jeremy.

He listened intently; his eyes never left her face. He did not even make his usual noises. Had he understood what she had said about Jesus' death and resurrection? Did he understand the assignment? Perhaps she should call his parents and explain the project to them.

That evening, Ms. Miller's kitchen sink stopped up. She called the landlord and waited an hour for him to come by and unclog the drain. After that, she still had to shop for groceries, iron a blouse, and prepare a vocabulary test for the next day. She had completely forgotten about phoning Jeremy's parents.

The next morning, nineteen children came to school, laughing and talking as they placed their eggs in the large wicker basket on Ms. Miller's desk. After they completed their math lesson, it was time to open the eggs. In the first egg, there was a flower.

"Oh yes, a flower is certainly a sign of new life," she said.

"When plants peek through the ground, we know that spring is here."

A small girl in the first row waved her arm.

"That's my egg, Ms. Miller," she called out.

The next egg contained a plastic butterfly, which looked very real. Doris held it up.

"We all know that a caterpillar changes and grows into a beautiful butterfly. Yes, that's new life too."

Little Judy smiled proudly and said, "Ms. Miller, that one is mine."

The next egg had a rock with moss on it. She explained that moss, too, showed life.

Billy spoke up from the back of the classroom, "My daddy helped me," he beamed.

Then Ms. Miller opened the fourth egg. She gasped. The egg was empty. Surely, it must be Jeremy's, she thought, and of course, he did not understand her instructions. If only she had not forgotten to phone his parents. Because she did not want to embarrass him, she quietly set the egg aside and reached for another. Suddenly, Jeremy spoke up.

"Ms. Miller, aren't you going to talk about my egg?"

Flustered, Ms. Miller replied, "But Jeremy, your egg is empty."

He looked into her eyes and said softly, "Yes, but Jesus's tomb was empty too."

Time stopped. When she could speak again, Ms. Miller asked him, "Do you know why the tomb was empty?"

"Oh, yes," Jeremy said. "Jesus was killed and put in there. Then His Father raised Him up."

The recess bell rang. While the children excitedly ran out to the schoolyard, Ms. Miller cried. The cold inside her melted completely away.

Three months later, Jeremy died. Those who paid their respects at the mortuary were surprised to see nineteen eggs on top of his casket, all of them empty.

—*Author unknown*

Life is good

1. Give people more than they expect, and do it cheerfully.
2. Memorize your favorite poem.
3. Don't believe all you hear, spend all you have, or loaf all you want.
4. When you say, "I love you," mean it.
5. When you say, "I'm sorry," look the person in the eye.
6. Be engaged at least six months before you get married.
7. Believe in love at first sight.
8. Never laugh at anyone's dreams. People who don't have dreams don't have much.
9. Love deeply and passionately. You may get hurt, but it's the only way to live life completely.
10. In disagreements, fight fairly. No name-calling.
11. Don't judge people by their relatives or by the life they were born into.
12. Teach yourself to speak slowly but think quickly.
13. When someone asks you a question you don't want to answer, smile and ask, "Why do you want to know?"
14. Take into account that great love and great achievements involve great risk.
15. Call your mother.
16. Say "bless you" when you hear someone sneeze.
17. When you lose, don't lose the lesson.
18. Follow the three Rs: respect for self, respect for others, and responsibility for all your actions.
19. Don't let a little dispute injure a great friendship.
20. When you realize you've made a mistake, take immediate steps to correct it.
21. Smile when picking up the phone. The caller will hear it in your voice.
22. Marry a person you love to talk to. As you get older, their conversational skills will be even more important.
23. Spend some time alone.
24. Open your arms to change, but don't let go of your values.

25. Remember that silence is sometimes the best answer.
26. Read more books. Television is no substitute.
27. Live a good, honorable life. Then when you get older and think back, you'll be able to enjoy it a second time.
28. Trust in God, but lock your car.
29. A loving atmosphere in your home is the foundation for your life. Do all you can to create a tranquil, harmonious home.
30. In disagreements with loved ones, deal only with the current situation. Don't bring up the past.
31. Don't just listen to what someone is saying. Listen to why they are saying it.
32. Share your knowledge. It's a way to achieve immortality.
33. Be gentle with the earth.
34. Pray or meditate. There's immeasurable power in it.
35. Never interrupt when you are being flattered.
36. Mind your own business.
37. Don't trust anyone who doesn't close their eyes when you kiss.
38. Once a year, go someplace you've never been before.
39. If you make a lot of money, put it to use helping others while you are living. It is wealth's greatest satisfaction.
40. Remember that not getting what you want is sometimes a wonderful stroke of luck.
41. Learn the rules so you know how to break them properly.
42. Remember that the best relationship is one in which your love for each other exceeds your need for each other.
43. Judge your success by what you have to give up.
44. Live with the knowledge that your character is your destiny.
45. Approach love and cooking with reckless abandon.

—Author unknown

Little tidbits

- Black holes are where God divided by zero.

- All those who believe in psychokinesis raise my hand.
- Early bird gets the worm, but the second mouse gets the cheese.
- Quantum Mechanics: The dreams stuff is made of.
- I almost had a psychic girlfriend, but she left me before we met.
- How do you tell when you run out of invisible ink?
- Support bacteria—they're the only culture some people have.
- Depression is merely anger without enthusiasm.
- When everything's coming your way, you're in the wrong lane.
- Ambition is a poor excuse for not having enough sense to be lazy.
- Hard work pays off in the future. Laziness pays off now.
- The only substitute for good manners is fast reflexes.
- Everyone has a photographic memory. Some don't have film.
- Shin: a device for finding furniture in the dark.
- Many people quit looking for work when they find a job.
- I intend to live forever—so far, so good.
- Join the Army, meet interesting people, kill them.
- Energizer Bunny was arrested and charged with battery.
- If Barbie is so popular, why do you have to buy her friends?
- Eagles may soar, but weasels don't get sucked into jet engines.
- I drive way too fast to worry about cholesterol.
- I love defenseless animals, especially in a good gravy.
- If you ain't makin' waves, you ain't kickin' hard enough!
- If I worked as much as others, I would do as little as they.
- What happens if you get scared half to death twice?
- I poured Spot Remover on my dog. Now he's gone.
- I used to have an open mind, but my brains kept falling out.
- Laughing stock: cattle with a sense of humor.
- Why do psychics have to ask you for your name?

- If at first you don't succeed, destroy all evidence that you tried.
- If at first you don't succeed, then skydiving definitely isn't for you.
- A conclusion is the place where you get tired of thinking.
- Experience is something you don't get until just after you need it.
- For every action, there is an equal and opposite criticism.
- He who hesitates is probably right.
- No one is listening until you make a mistake.
- Success always occurs in private, and failure in full view.
- To steal ideas from one person is plagiarism; to steal from many is "research."
- Change is inevitable…except from vending machines.
- Plan to be spontaneous tomorrow.
- Always try to be modest. And be *very* proud of it!
- If you think nobody cares about you, try missing a couple of payments.
- Attempt to get a new car for your spouse—it'll be a great trade!
- Everybody, repeat after me: "We are all individuals."
- I'd kill for a Nobel Peace Prize.
- Borrow money from pessimists. They don't expect it back.
- Half the people you know are below average.
- Ninety-nine percent of lawyers give the rest a bad name.
- About 42.7 percent of all statistics are made up on the spot.

ABOUT THE AUTHOR

Raised in Kansas, Ellen Weber Newlin is a wife, mother, grandmother, homemaker, and retired secretary. The Newlins also lived and worked in New York and Oklahoma. On a side note, Ellen and her husband served as short-term missionaries in Dunfermline, Scotland. The Newlins enjoy traveling and spending time with their children and grandchildren. This publication has been an exciting adventure.

Printed in the USA
CPSIA information can be obtained
at www.ICGtesting.com
CBHW051232151124
17428CB00006B/855